THE WORLD OF HOBBIES

HOBBIES IF YOU LIKE NATURE

by Sue Bradford Edwards

BrightPoint Press

San Diego, CA

I0869414

BrightPoint Press

© 2025 BrightPoint Press
an imprint of ReferencePoint Press, Inc.
Printed in the United States

For more information, contact:
BrightPoint Press
PO Box 27779
San Diego, CA 92198
www.BrightPointPress.com

ALL RIGHTS RESERVED.
No part of this work covered by the copyright hereon may be reproduced or used in any form or by any means—graphic, electronic, or mechanical, including photocopying, recording, taping, web distribution, or information storage retrieval systems—without the written permission of the publisher.

LIBRARY OF CONGRESS CATALOGING-IN-PUBLICATION DATA

Name: Edwards, Sue Bradford, author.
Title: Hobbies If You Like Nature / by Sue Bradford Edwards.
Description: San Diego, CA: ReferencePoint Press, Inc., 2025 | Series: The World of Hobbies | Audience: Grade 6 to 12 | Includes bibliographical references and index.
Identifiers: ISBN: 9781678208844 (hardcover) | ISBN: 9781678208851 (eBook)
The complete Library of Congress record is available at www.loc.gov.

CONTENTS

AT A GLANCE

- Birding involves looking for different types of birds. Many birders use binoculars and guidebooks.

- People can go birding in cities or in wilderness areas. Some people join birding groups or use birding apps on their phones.

- A kayak is a small boat that sits low in the water. Kayakers control the boat with a double-sided paddle.

- Kayaking requires special gear and safety skills. Some state parks and outdoor gear stores offer kayaking classes for beginners.

- Geocaching involves searching for hidden items using Global Positioning System (GPS) coordinates. People search for a cache, or collection of items.

- Geocachers can choose easy-to-find caches or more advanced ones. When they find a cache, they sign a logbook and take a piece of swag from the cache.

- Hiking involves exploring the natural world on foot. People can choose hiking trails based on their length and level of difficulty. Hikers may need gear such as backpacks, water, jackets, and a compass.

- Camping involves staying overnight in an outdoor shelter. Many people camp in a tent, camper, or car. They may bring equipment for cooking outside.

CITY BIRDS

Maya's mom parked the car in a lot at Forest Park. The sun had just begun to set. "Maya, did you take off your earmuffs?" she asked.

"I'm wearing a beanie," Maya said. When she and her parents went winter birding, it was important to dress warmly. Normally, Maya wore fluffy earmuffs. But today, she and her parents weren't going on just any birding adventure. They were going on an

To spot birds, people must pay close attention to their surroundings. Many people use binoculars to view birds that are far away.

Many local parks, state parks, and wildlife areas host birding tours. People can go birding with an experienced guide.

owl prowl. This meant no one could wear any clothing with fur on it. It also meant dogs had to stay home. Maya knew this was because owls are **predators**. An owl might attack a small dog. It might think furry earmuffs are a small animal.

Near the parking lot, ten people gathered around a man. "I'm Mark," the man said. "I'll be your guide today. Since you are all new to the owl prowl, let me go over a few things." After he explained the rules, the group was ready to go.

"Does everyone have their binoculars?" Mark asked. "We'll have to take a short hike to get to where I saw the owls. They move their nests regularly. If you come next week, the owls will probably be in a new place."

LOOKING FOR OWLS

The group followed Mark down the park trail. As they walked, Maya heard the hum of cars. The highway was less than a mile away. Forest Park lay in the middle of St. Louis, Missouri. It included a zoo and several museums. But the park was still home to a variety of wildlife. Maya hoped they would get to see some great horned owls.

Mark stopped and gestured toward a stand of trees. “The owls should be just waking up,” he said. “They will be getting ready to hunt.”

Maya looked through her binoculars. First, she looked down toward the base of the trees. Then she looked up. “I think I see something on that high branch,” she said.

“That’s the male owl stretching,” said Mark. “We call him Charles.”

“He’s so big,” Maya whispered. “Look at those wings,” whispered Maya’s mom. The group stayed quiet to avoid scaring the

Birders learn the best times of day to see certain birds. Some owls, for example, are most active at dusk and dawn.

owl away. Maya kept her focus on the bird. A moment later, it silently flew out of sight.

Maya took out her birding notebook. She added the owl to the list of birds she'd seen. She hoped to come back to the park soon to see the owls again.

CHAPTER ONE

BIRDING

Birding, or bird-watching, is a hobby that nature lovers can do almost anywhere. "You can do it through your home or car window, while taking a rigorous hike, or anything in-between. I know bike riders who bird while biking," says Rich Merritt.[1] Merritt works for Audubon New York. This organization focuses on bird **conservation**.

Many people watch birds in their backyards. They put out bird feeders and

Birders can hang different types of bird feeders to attract a variety of birds. They might fill bird feeders with seeds or nuts.

water to attract birds. Then they watch and listen to birds that come. Many birders **identify** the birds they see. They add the names of the birds to their life list. This is a list of all the different birds that a birder has seen. The list grows whenever they spot a new type of bird.

GETTING STARTED

To get started with birding, people need several basic tools. One important piece of gear is a pair of binoculars. Binoculars allow people to see things that are far away. They have two eyepieces, one for each eye. A good pair of binoculars is sturdy enough to not break if they are dropped. Binoculars should also be light enough for a birder to wear around their neck on a strap.

Birders also need a guidebook. When birders spot a bird, they look it up in the guidebook. The book contains information about different types of birds. This may include the colors, sounds, or **habitats** of a bird. Birders use this information to identify birds they see. Identifying birds can be tricky. Male and female cardinals, for example, are different colors. A flying

Binoculars by the Numbers

Birders need good binoculars. Quality birding binoculars are usually 8x42. The first number means the binoculars make things look eight times closer than they are. The second number is the width of the larger lens. A standard lens measurement is 42 millimeters (1.7 in). Bigger numbers mean larger lenses and heavier binoculars.

Birding guidebooks are also called field guides. People often carry them while birding. This way, they can easily identify any birds they see.

bird may look different than the same bird perched on a branch. A good birding guidebook will include several pictures of each bird **species**. The Sibley guides are popular. National and state park gift shops often sell birding guides. They can also be purchased at bookstores.

Some birders use birding apps. People at Cornell University created an app called Merlin. It has regional "bird packs." These lists help birders know which birds live in their area. Apps also make it easy to look up birds by behavior. For instance,

The National Audubon Society marks specific habitats around the world as Important Bird Areas. These are popular places for birding.

birds might be listed as perching birds or wading birds.

BIRDING GROUPS

Joining a birding group is a good way to begin birding. With a group, new birders can learn the best places to look for specific birds. They can learn to identify different bird songs. The National Audubon Society helps people locate birding clubs in their area. People can also look up birding groups online.

The Missouri Young Birders Club has groups in several Missouri cities. They lead birding hikes and teach people how to recognize birds. They also restore bird habitats.

EXPLORING THE OUTDOORS

Once birders know the basics, some go birding alone. This makes it easy to get outside and explore at any time. Many types of birds are easiest to find first thing in the morning. That's when they sing, chirp, and feed.

At Santa Monica Mountains National Recreation Area in California, beginners can join park rangers for birding walks.

New birders don't have to travel far. City dwellers can start birding in their own neighborhoods. "All you have to do is to get your head around the idea that birds and other wildlife are everywhere," David Lindo says.[2] Lindo is a birder and author.

Some birders take photos of birds they see. They may use special cameras and equipment.

He teaches city people how to engage with wildlife where they live.

There are many benefits to birding. One is that it gives people a chance to explore. Many birds like big trees. Some nest in shrubs. Others prefer areas around lakes. Birding is also good for people. Scientists have found that walking and listening to birds promotes good health. It reduces stress. Going birding can help relieve depression and anxiety. And with each new bird, a birder's life list grows.

CHAPTER TWO

KAYAKING

Kayaking is a great hobby for people who enjoy the outdoors. A kayak is a small boat that can fit one or two people. The kayaker uses a paddle with a blade on each end. They paddle on one side of the kayak and then the other. This moves the boat forward. Kayakers can explore lakes and rivers. Kayaking can also be combined with other outdoor activities, such as camping or fishing.

Kayaking is a way for people to spend time outdoors and explore new places. It can also be a good workout.

In kayaking classes, experts teach people how to kayak safely and use equipment properly. They may also offer tips about paddling techniques.

There are three types of kayaking. These are recreational kayaking, sport kayaking, and sea kayaking. Recreational kayaking is calm and easy. It allows people to stop and appreciate nature. It is a good way to explore shallow waters at the edges of lakes. Sport kayaking is more athletic. It involves racing or kayaking through white water rapids. Rapids occur where rivers flow quickly over rocks. Sea kayaking is the most challenging. It requires a heavy-duty sea kayak. This type of kayak is longer than other kayaks. It also has more storage space. Sea kayaking trips may last up to a week. Sometimes kayakers go whale watching on these trips.

GETTING STARTED

New kayakers have a lot to learn. They must learn how to safely launch and land their kayaks. They must learn how to paddle. A kayaker must also practice what to do if their kayak **capsizes**. Beginners can take a class or go on an outing with a club. REI is a chain of stores that sells outdoor gear. It offers kayaking classes and tours. Many state parks also offer classes.

Missouri State Parks offers a class called Learn2 Paddle. In 2023, the class cost only five dollars.

New kayakers don't need to buy their own boats. Rental kayaks are available at many lakes. This means people don't need to transport their own boats. When someone rents a kayak, they get a paddle and personal flotation device, too. A personal floatation device is also called a PFD or life jacket. If a person's kayak tips, the PFD keeps them afloat. Dan Arbuckle ran the store Headwaters Kayak. He recommends getting "a paddling specific PFD."[3] This is a PFD with arm cutouts that are deep enough to avoid **chafing**. That can help make paddling easier.

KAYAKING GEAR

New kayakers need other types of gear, too. They should wear waterproof shoes and clothes that can get wet. A hat and sunscreen are also important. Kayakers may also need a dry bag to protect their cell phones from water. If a person is kayaking later in the day, they should bring

Safety First

Sometimes new kayakers don't wear their PFDs. But safety is very important while kayaking. Ken Whiting is a professional kayaker and kayaking teacher. He appears on the PaddleTV YouTube channel. "Wear the life jacket and wear it properly so that if you do go for a swim, it is ready to do its job," says Whiting.

Quoted in PaddleTV, "Top 5 Kayaking Mistakes," YouTube, *August 2, 2022, www.youtube.com.*

a headlamp with extra batteries. To stay safe, a kayaker should also bring a whistle. They can use it to signal for help if they get lost or separated from their group.

Some kayakers buy bilge pumps. Water often gets into a kayak. This makes the kayak heavier and harder to paddle. It can also mean the kayaker is sitting in cold water. Some people use a bilge pump to pump water out of their boat.

WHY KAYAK?

People choose kayaking as a hobby for many different reasons. It is a great way to explore the outdoors and spend time with other nature lovers. It also provides good exercise. Kayaking can be a workout for the arms, shoulders, and core. But many

Many schools and recreation centers offer kayaking programs for kids and teens.

people also find it relaxing. Spending hours on the water can be a way to de-stress.

Kayaking is also fun to do with others. Young kayakers can join school clubs. They might also find kayaking programs at local or state parks. There are even online forums about kayaking. Kayaking can be inexpensive, too. People can save money by renting a boat or buying a used one.

CHAPTER THREE

GEOCACHING

Geocaching is like a modern-day treasure hunt. It involves searching for hidden items using Global Positioning System (GPS) **coordinates**. First, someone hides a cache, or collection of items. Then other people try to find the items.

The term *geocache* combines *geo*, meaning earth, with the word *cache*. But cache is also a computer term for memory

People can go geocaching alone or with a group. To stay safe, beginners should stick with their group and stay on marked trails.

People can use Geocaching.com to locate caches and track how many they've found. The app also provides navigation tools and hints.

or storage. Geocaching involves both technology and geography.

HOW IT WORKS

To get started, beginners can sign up for a free account at Geocaching.com. Then they download a geocaching app onto their smartphone. Using the app, the geocacher chooses a cache in their area. There are different levels of difficulty. Beginners can choose easy-to-find caches. More experienced geocachers can choose advanced ones. An easy-to-find cache may be secured to the bottom of a bench. It may be hidden among tree roots. A more difficult cache may be disguised as a mushroom. It may be hidden inside a brick or post.

The app gives the geocacher the coordinates of a location within 30 feet (9 m) of the cache. Some caches are in urban areas. People may be able to reach them by simply walking down a city sidewalk. Other caches require hiking through a state park.

Once the geocacher finds the cache, they sign a logbook. This book is hidden with the cache. It is important to do this without revealing the cache's location to others. Steve Wood is an instructor at REI Outdoor School. He recommends that geocachers bring the cache away from the hiding area so they "can go ahead and look at it without exposing the hiding spot to anyone who's not involved in the game."[4] Then the geocacher can choose one of the items in the cache. These items are called swag.

BASIC GEAR

New geocachers need several pieces of gear. They must have a smartphone to view the geocaching map. Additional gear varies depending on the location of the cache. Most geocachers wear a good pair of

There are many types of cache containers, including metal boxes, canisters, and clear bins. People can buy cache kits and containers on Geocaching.com.

walking or hiking shoes. Depending on the weather, they may also need sunscreen, a hat, or a rain jacket. If a cache is hidden in a wilderness area, players may need hiking or camping gear. A map and compass may be needed, too. Cell signals aren't available in all rural areas.

Geocachers should also bring a pen or pencil to sign the logbook. Some people may bring a headlamp. This is helpful if a cache takes a long time to find.

Geocachers should bring swag, too. That's one of the basic geocaching rules. Taking swag is a trade. To take a piece

Caches may contain all kinds of swag items, such as keychains or small toys. Some also contain stickers, coins, or bracelets.

of swag from the cache, a geocacher must leave something behind. Many caches contain items such as keychains or small plastic toys. Some people leave a trackable. This is an item that people transfer from cache to cache. It has a code on it. Geocachers log the code to track the item's journey.

Trackables

Trackables may be customized coins called geocoins. Some are travel bugs, or special tags. Trackables include six-digit tracking codes. They often have goals printed on them. The goal says where the trackable's creator wants it to end up. For example, a goal might say "Take me to the beach." A player who can help takes the trackable to a cache closer to the goal. They record this movement on Geocaching.com.

Geocaching can be a good way to practice using a map and compass. It can also build problem-solving skills and teamwork.

WHY PLAY?

Geocaching.com asked hobbyists about why they geocache. People gave a wide variety of answers. Some people said geocaching is a fun way to spend time outside. Others said the hobby is a way to make friends, explore, and travel. Some players enjoy seeing how different people hide their caches.

Many people think geocaching is a great way to clean up the environment. Geocachers try to follow the "leave no trace" rule. This means people should not leave litter in natural areas. They shouldn't damage the environment. Instead, they should leave natural areas exactly as they found them. Many players pick up any litter they find while geocaching.

HIKING

Hiking is all about walking in nature. It is often part of other outdoor hobbies, including mountain climbing and birding. Hikers carry their gear. They may hike for an hour, a day, or several days. Multi-day hikes often require camping along the way. Hiking can be a great way to get closer to nature.

Bob and Martha Manning work with the American Hiking Society. They encourage people to hike. They say new hikers should

To stay safe, beginners should go hiking with a partner or in a group. They should start with beginner-friendly hikes on familiar trails.

Some national and state parks offer guided hikes. At Denali National Park in Alaska, people can go on hikes with park rangers.

think about what types of hikes they like best. "Walk your own walk, not the walk that someone else thinks you should do," they say.[5] One person might enjoy long backpacking trips. Another may prefer more relaxed hikes. They want time to explore. Some people hike from one town to the next. They find comfortable places to stay instead of camping.

GETTING STARTED

Many people enjoy hiking on their own. But beginners should always hike with an experienced friend. They can also join a hiking club or sign up for a guided hike. Little Jerusalem Badlands State Park is in Kansas. Hikers can go on guided hikes at the park. This gives them a chance to learn

Trail Etiquette

On narrow hiking trails, it is important to know who should step aside. When two hikers meet, the hiker going downhill should step aside to let the other person pass. Mountain bikers should yield to hikers. But bikes move fast. It is often easier for hikers to step aside first. When meeting a horse, a hiker should step aside.

about local wildlife. They also learn about the park's rock formations. Guided hikes help new hikers stay safe while learning the basics.

To plan a hike, a person must pick a trail. Many state parks have hiking trails. One example is the Skyline Trail in Davis Mountains State Park in Texas. People can also search online for trails. Trails have various lengths and levels of difficulty.

Hikers should think about how far and long they want to hike. A long hike may be impossible for someone who only has a few hours. Fitness is another factor. Hiking on level ground is easier than hiking uphill. The weather matters, too. In summer, hikers may need to prepare for extreme heat. In winter, they must prepare for the cold.

POPULAR HIKING TRAILS

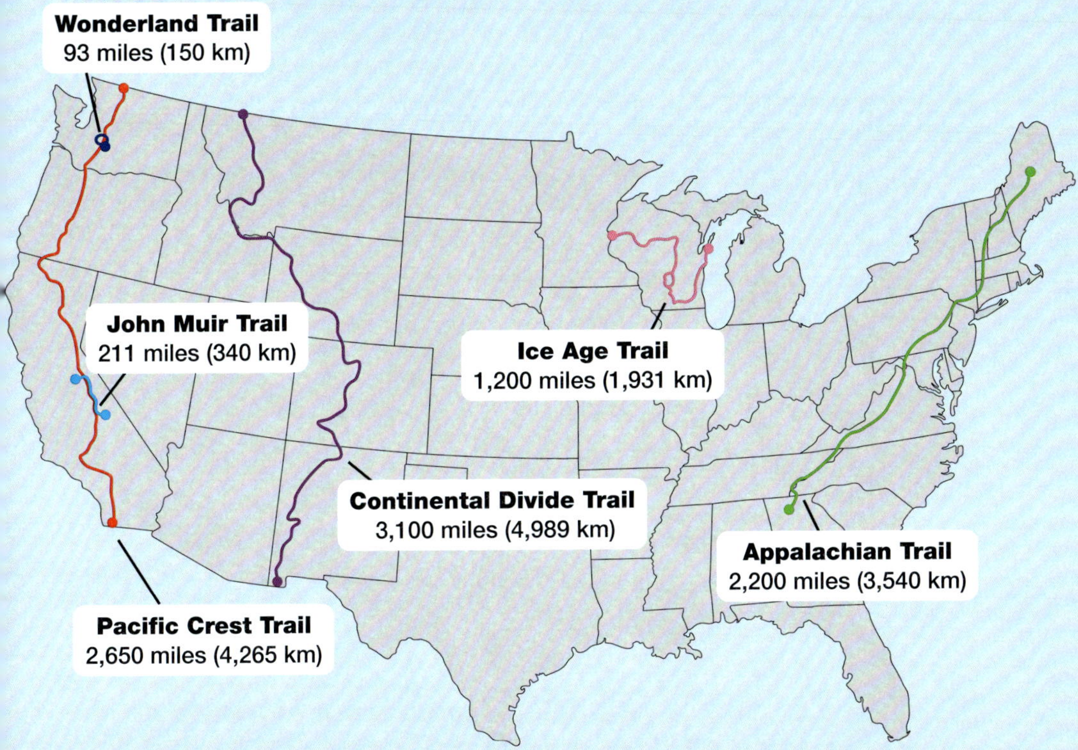

Source: "Map: America's Best Long Trails," Backpacker, *March 18, 2024. www.backpacker.com.*

There are many popular hiking trails across the United States. Some trails are very long.

ESSENTIAL GEAR

Hikers need the right gear. A pair of hiking boots or trail shoes is essential. Hikers should wear **synthetic** or wool socks. These keep their feet dry. They help hikers avoid getting blisters. It is a good idea to wear layers of clothing while hiking. In cold weather, hikers often need a base layer, such as long underwear. This layer lies close to the skin, keeping the hiker warm. Gloves, hats, and jackets may also be necessary. In summer, hikers can wear hats to protect themselves from the sun.

Many hikers wear special hiking boots or shoes. These help hikers keep their footing on rocky, uneven trails.

Many hikers carry backpacks, too. They use these to hold snacks, a jacket, and water bottles. Some hikers also carry water treatment kits. If they get lost or run out of water, they can purify water they find. A first aid kit is essential in case someone falls or gets hurt. Toilet paper and a plastic bag are helpful, too. The plastic bag can hold used toilet paper.

THE POSITIVES

Many people enjoy getting to know others through hiking. They enjoy spending time outdoors. Many hikers join groups such as the Wilderness Society. This group helps maintain trails. It helps hikers find lodging and safe hiking spots. The Appalachian Trail Conference works with groups in fourteen states. It maintains campsites along the Appalachian Trail. This trail runs from Maine to Georgia. It is 2,200 miles (3,540 km) long.

People also enjoy hiking because it is an affordable way to get exercise. People can pick the terrain and difficulty of their hikes. They can choose short, easy walks or long, hilly hikes. Preparation is key. "The more prepared you are, the easier it is to switch from day hikes to overnight trips," says author and hiker Shawnté Salabert.[6] Planning hikes builds confidence and skill.

Hiking is a good way to stay active and spend time outdoors. It can also improve a person's mental health.

CHAPTER FIVE

CAMPING

Camping is a great hobby for people who enjoy spending time outside. It involves staying overnight in an outdoor shelter. Some people stay in campers, or RVs. These truck-like vehicles often have spaces for cooking, sleeping, and bathing. Some people sleep in their cars while camping. Others sleep in tents.

There are many ways to camp. Some people prefer to stay in small tents. They go

Camping is a great way to get outdoors and spend time with friends and family. People can go camping alone or in groups.

hiking and fishing. They cook food over a campfire. Other people camp in luxury. Large campers may have beds and kitchens. A roof can be pulled out of the camper for shelter. People may also bring outdoor tables and chairs for dining.

GETTING STARTED

New campers can learn the basics by taking a class. Many community centers and outdoor gear stores offer camping classes. REI hosts classes and workshops about camping. In REI's Beginner's Camping Workshop, people learn to set up tents. They learn how to choose the right type of sleeping bag. Beginners can also gain basic skills by going camping with an experienced camper.

Camping classes can help people choose the right type of tent and learn how to set it up properly at their campsite.

Camping requires a wide variety of gear. One of the first things people need is a tent. Some tents are very small, fitting only two people. Others are large enough for six people. Some tents are even big enough for someone to stand inside. Beginners should practice putting up their tent before going camping. This will make setting up camp at the campsite faster and easier.

Sleeping bags and pads are also essential for camping. People need the right kind of bag and pad. According to the REI website, "A good sleeping pad provides comfort, but it also has high-tech insulation to prevent you from losing body heat to the cold ground."[7]

Campers must also think about how they will prepare food. Not all people enjoy cooking over a fire. Some bring food in a cooler. Others want to cook outdoors. They bring portable cooking equipment, such as a camp stove.

CAMPING GEAR AND SAFETY

Campers need other gear, too. They should bring a lantern and batteries. They may need sunscreen, insect repellent, and a first aid kit. A map and compass can help people avoid getting lost. It's important to pack clothing for all types of weather, too. Campers may want to wear hats and shorts in summer. In winter, they will likely need warm jackets and gloves.

New campers often want to tough it out no matter what. But safety comes first. Sometimes people must cancel a camping trip if the weather becomes cold or stormy.

Food Safety

Animals often visit campsites looking for food. Campers should store food and trash in latching bins or coolers. Storing them in the trunk of a car also works. This helps people avoid attracting wildlife to their campsite. Bears require greater precautions. In areas with bears, campers hang food in trees. Others store it in bear-safe canisters or sacks.

Campers may prepare food with equipment such as camping stoves. They may bring cooking utensils such as spatulas, spoons, pots, and bowls.

WHY CAMP?

Many people who camp enjoy spending time in the fresh air. They get to experience nature and see wildlife. Camping can lower stress levels, too. This is because campers don't have to stick to a schedule. They aren't interrupted. They can relax away from their busy lives.

The camping experience can also benefit a person's mental health. The National Park Service says camping can help people take a break from phones and TV screens. It says, "These places are perfect locations to put down the digital devices in our lives and focus on the basics that we still have access to. Sit back and relax with a good book, draw in a sketchbook, or write in a journal."[8]

There are a wide variety of hobbies for people who enjoy nature. Outdoor hobbies are a great way to get up, get outside, and be active. People with these hobbies often find friends with similar interests. Whether a person is hiking or birding, the great outdoors is full of adventures and activities for everyone.

GLOSSARY

capsizes

tips over in water

chafing

rubbing that leads to sore skin

conservation

the act of preserving and protecting natural resources

coordinates

numerical points that mark a geographic location

habitats

the homes of plants or animals

identify

to name what something is

predators

animals that eat other animals

species

a group of animals or plants that share the same characteristics and can produce offspring

synthetic

describing a fabric made from manufactured materials

SOURCE NOTES

CHAPTER ONE: BIRDING

1. Quoted in "Bird Watching 101: A Guide for Beginners," *Audubon New York*, n.d. ny.audubon.org.

2. David Lindo, "The Act of Urban Birding," *YouTube*, September 24, 2018. www.youtube.com.

CHAPTER TWO: KAYAKING

3. Dan Arbuckle, "5 Mistakes Every New Kayaker Makes . . . And How to Avoid Them," *YouTube*, July 21, 2022. www.youtube.com.

CHAPTER THREE: GEOCACHING

4. Steve Wood, "Navigation Expert Advice: Introduction to Geocaching," *YouTube*, November 16, 2016. www.youtube.com.

CHAPTER FOUR: HIKING

5. Quoted in "#HikingMakesMe Interview – Bob and Martha Manning," *American Hiking Society,* n.d. americanhiking.org.

6. Quoted in Jeff Hester, "Interview with Shawnté Salabert, Author of Hiking the Pacific Crest Trail – Southern California," *SoCal Hiker*, November 3, 2017. socalhiker.net.

CHAPTER FOUR: CAMPING

7. Quoted in "Camping for Beginners," *REI*, n.d. www.rei.com.

8. Quoted in "Why Camp?" *National Park Service*, June 5, 2019. www.nps.gov.

FOR FURTHER RESEARCH

BOOKS

Patricia Hutchison, *Boating*. Minneapolis, MN: Abdo, 2020.

Donna B. McKinney, *Camping*. Minneapolis, MN: Abdo, 2020.

Barbara Taylor, *The Bird Atlas*. New York: DK, 2021.

INTERNET SOURCES

"Geocaching," *National Geographic*, October 19, 2023. education.nationalgeographic.org.

"Hiking," *Britannica Kids*, n.d. kids.britannica.com.

"Why Camp?" *National Park Service*, June 5, 2019. nps.gov.

WEBSITES

Geocaching.com
www.geocaching.com

Geocaching.com is the official site for geocaching. It provides information for beginners and tips for finding hidden caches.

National Audubon Society
www.audubon.org

The National Audubon Society is an organization dedicated to protecting birds and their habitats. Its website provides detailed information about different types of birds.

National Park Service (NPS)
nps.gov

The National Park Service maintains national parks throughout the United States. Its website provides a list of parks, along with information about hiking, camping, and other outdoor activities.

INDEX

IMAGE CREDITS

Cover: © Drazen Zigic/Shutterstock Images
5: © LightField Studios/Shutterstock Images
7: © Lena_Viridis/Shutterstock Images
8: © Michael G. McKinne/Shutterstock Images
11: © Vlad G./Shutterstock Images
13: © Vishnevskiy Vasily/Shutterstock Images
16: © Rosyid A. Azhar/Shutterstock Images
17: © Tada Images/Shutterstock Images
19: © National Park Service
20: © Brian Lasenby/Shutterstock Images
23: © Scott Sharaga/National Park Service
24: © Geartooth Productions/Shutterstock Images
29: © B. Brown/Shutterstock Images
31: © Fertnig/iStockphoto
32: © M-Sur/Shutterstock Images
35: © G7Davies/Shutterstock Images
36: © Lucie Parizkova/Shutterstock Images
38: © Rawpixel.com/Shutterstock Images
41: © SeventyFour/Shutterstock Images
42: © Emily Mesner/National Park Service
45: © Red Line Editorial
46: © Zbynek Pospisil/iStockphoto
49: © SolStock/iStockphoto
51: © Ground Picture/Shutterstock Images
53: © Svetlaya_Strana_Omsk/Shutterstock Images
56: © Rawpixel.com/Shutterstock Images

ABOUT THE AUTHOR

Sue Bradford Edwards is a nonfiction author who lives in Missouri. She is the author of several Brightpoint Press titles, including *Become a Construction Equipment Operator*, *What Are Learning Disorders?*, and *Robotics in Healthcare*. She grew up wandering the hills and forests of Missouri. Every winter, she goes birding to see bald eagles nesting.